Euclid Shudders

Euclid Shudders

BY

MARK TARDI

Two parallel lines, being straight lines in the same plane and produced indefinitely in both directions, may never converge.

Euclid, *Definition 23*

LITMUS PRESS

BROOKLYN • 2003

Excerpts from this book have appeared previously—though sometimes in earlier forms—in the following publications: *Aufgabe, BlueSky, Issues, L'Bourgeoizine, Magazine Cypress, Saracen, syllogism, Upstairs at Duroc,* and *Washington Square Review.* I am grateful to the editors for their kindness and generosity.

ISBN: 0-9723331-2-6

Cover art & design by Miriam Kienle
Typesetting & book design by E. Tracy Grinnell

www.durationpress.com/litmuspress

Distributed by Small Press Distribution
1341 Seventh St. Berkeley, CA 94710

For those countless cups of tea . . .

Contents

Euclid Shudders

What is the difference
between arithmetic and a noun.

Gertrude Stein, "Sentences"

series 2

instead of entrance
Goodbye means *Avoir*

Sved's dream said from nowhere

of aliquant angles

some spindle of the sun

empirically facted
deafening skin

open and afterwards

a cough is a couch
idled into

without rain
an island

easily a third worse

Indigo with a flame-red tongue

series 3

Square 27 is the watertrap

subspatial island south
of the sentence

so well removed
everything took place at all

Often at times

anaerobes at
each upturned sheet

though under a residual *cers*

forwarded into hands
starved chairs

among partial hinges
clamps

that people might metaplasm

series 6

A squirrel is a swan

anaerobes at
each upturned sheet

if cloying meant

nose-coats
turn toward the slope

spondylolytic eclipse

allegedly strewn
at a point

carved with cups

an aisle
exacting date

In advance of the arm

margent ice ovens

between two breaths
of sun

series 7

"Scavenger's wrest"

At the sixth attempt at seven

a hand of mouths

clavicylindric leticuli

in every interstice

its division the moon

movable sticks or musculature

chimera in F-sharp minor

shoved against an echo

calcined cups

itch into the open

splinter spring

as if at any point incunable

series 11

svelte a swarm of flies

hairs breath parcelled in perfect eclipse

some other spring

bleeding sand
a dream of the lawn

antecubital étude

on a bridge
emptied with inertia

so close

canopic jars torn
beneath

scrept an imprecise skid

series 12

"asymmetrical echo"

nearly two mouths flee through a yawn

peroneous anti-stones

of the tumeric sequence

melting at an atmosphere

worn shadows

alibi an isotope

or lintel into grift

Today's dream was the color of subtraction. A violin in a void. But boats made of dust? The isotropic fuselage? There was a project for the sun and is. It's very. An octonary impulse or elbow for an ear. Yet one went and came and never claimed a bat for a bedroom. Without residue. Steady stairs to marrel the marcee. All weathers. Worn shadows thrown at length.

series 17

"violin in a void"

A decade doubled with grace

canting limbs
in a clock of ice

torn into tourniquets

horse mountains
misbled by

another lamplight

multiplied marks

roping breath
of its own accord

the moon removed

without residue
stone hunger

shuttled among subsmiles

another lamplight

roped breath
between late marks

agilant purls

or a tride of trees
unhinged

to burnish pulse

counter-conjured
without amber

the drills dream
calmed into a frenzy

starving glass

made of string
baubled

by malmute cranes

that barely come up

Tense. It passed itself only to forget it moved.

series 26

"of the parallel fall"

Until static starts to fold

steep the window
with broken bloodstone

grapht fimbriate
shoreless

weathered in wire

the dream differential
craning distrobe

with equal aptness
niantic skin

off a measure

sewn into echoes

not even a breeze
inexorable sums

relative to the plane

series 29

Assemble its reciprocus

with a vacant knot
blood silence

disaffected by

weathered in wire

antic pillars
sunken skyward

the plastic velocity

otherwise unseen

folding sleep
between two keys

some indistant auricle

identical orphan
said with shorn eyes

The pivot chord is B$^{\flat\flat}$ which sounds as A in the new key of E. Folds of sleep between clouded and out loud. Its portion of night remains leaf-long and less than a foot away. A ladder of liquid. Or city forgetting to ask. Exactly like a statue. Old fires and profitable ghosts. A phrase worth repeating.

series 37

before slumber found a stone

the toric frequency

robed light
left at the piano

threadless
factorially stilled

unpronounced angles

the knock apparition
without

reference to its embedding

to build a blindspot
before voice

eyes swallowed hard

factorial rust
that holds up light

or ionatic arcs

if untouched after
almost absent

the alphabet alien

inside clock burns

sleep torn
binding celerity

breadthless length

pierced into spheres

series 43

"forgotten paper lantern of a strange color"

If it is not a shadow . . . a curtain

the floating horizon

or flecks of fur

beside the tubercle

the child slept its mouth

boats made of dust

intent with

an initial unknown

strangling scissors

and for hours

eyes swallowed hard

unlikely to invent auriform

or a surrender to zero

Unnumbered Poems

*An important, a
very important, a
frightening, a cataclysmic,
a frantic, a
good and evil
number.*

Keith Waldrop, from "An Excellent Guide"

speed trials

not an ogreless touch, lakes
elevated to rust

doubling as grace
delicate throats somewhat shapeless

"I dreamed today of a donkey that looked like a greyhound"

bound up in colored static

cascades of dust &
pretty burns

all pierced with arches beyond which
other arches opened

The distance of the moon at daybreak

still flat

either set of stains
cantilevered staircase

less a sandbox, cistern candles

carcasses on my feet
born between syllables

resembling a course
uncountable sets

In the open ledge of a fraction

Piece No. 2

It could be said Pascal had nothing to do with numbers.

For instance, a long dour face, a lined face

Solution A was "I would erase iridescence." Solution B "for
the desired amount under running water."

It's still hard to do.

The map said: trespass beyond the prearranged

splints of stars, blue nipples & geo-
metrical designs of the day. What

was left of the ring became a question
vortex sternposts

almost describing a circle

Roubaud's Law

if the 20 common to
the three floors is taken away
we are left with the series

semi-circles paral-
lel to wall openings

diaphanous body in
the stere of the door, a map in

a mirror (But I had
already planned to
write it elsewhere in a

location to be described
later) These are three conditions
which often look alike

This portion
of the broadcast
has been excerpted from

This portion
of the broadcast
is not really happening

All written recollections
disappear Only their blackened
trace is left behind, re-

verse eulogy Some people sitting

near the open space with certain colors
& a certain device *Tout condamné*
à mort aura la tête tranchée

(my head in the sawn off
cone of electric light

Perhaps the second Frédéric
is among the number

Bushalte 12

Go means melted nails,
fractals, sums of squares

Marie's death cry in Wozzeck
or that of Lulu

some irons eating

knees, toes, elbows:
these are also faces

at midnight—no longer a trade

less broken up here
between the arrow and needle
rock pools

All the waves that undulate through
such fields

Untitled (Henri-Chapelle)

You ask what the flowers said—They were disobedient

numeric cathedrals
coweringunderthevein

& the angle of something or other, I forgot what
without rain, bronze-armed but pierced.

We komen aan in Leuven

because the walls were flowers
in a field of stone

mud or else trees
surrounded by water

It didn't exist perhaps
in a direction equivalent to the sun

tank irrelevancy where birds took the shape of glass
and "Spring" postillions

J'ai toujours admiré l'œuvre
ormonde du sublime. And in the meantime the rain

had become a voluptuous tower.

59G

for Jeremy Giller

All the village clocks told October

If you are around when you go away

more than a leaf is missing
a ladder of liquid

between pins and piano aprons

or that shimmer of fog

But you must have been there
for the birth of midnight

bearing softly spoken eyes and
sky-shaped bread

with little more than abandon

motionless gestures melted into numbers

One looks like a tent
the other a cord of wool

Proposition (II/—)

predict S's popularity based on a rating of 5 and 8

such as six months' German, a molecular dance

Because you were to have found different counsel among the remains
Because you bore fragments of a face

namegiving in the shape of a vanishing point.

at different times a triangle equivalent to the sun in a direction
An example is an electrode

the hand, the sound that broke the back-of-words
composed of 13 flat feet

It and an arch
secondary calculations, notes and oscilate borders

> the Frames should be exactly
> but if it rains there is no water
> which would be a room
> grotesque vessels type
> O to its fullest expression
> (doubtless not like that at all)
> The color in question begins with of
> scarred corners aspice
> Rethberg Shark's Head and length
> Certain parts are not visible
> For instance, the S sound of abandon

Four Parenthetical Poems

I.

I am made sick in the right part of my forehead
the way water hacks up the street

II.

I used to think to when I died. So I died as fast as I could.

III.

"am I but feet?

IV.

I cannot ~~talk~~ (stay)
~~tonight~~ (now)

zH

The first word was Y. In the margin

he penned The dark leaves in my prose.

arms became visible, fall outside.

Between fire & fire

Spoke silent songs of *Planh*

Water is floating ash. In the margin

he penned A head growing from the

center of my face: burned bandages,

cornered cube, ornament & amulet

The dream marked the end of the dream

of which they are mere ghosts. Particulated

feet of statues, an ogress riddled with orifices

Did the cryptic dials & meters

in the courtyard, imbued or imparted.

At this rate you can go

You can afford to go at this rate

The turn behind the door

enchanted in two directions.

Peter Kaplan Sequence

*I shall have written with dust alone; for there are not
words, only the dust of lost characters from which we have
composed an alphabet.*

Edmond Jabès, *The Book of Margins*

Dear Peter,

It's possible there's a city inside me, and shards resemble frogs with paper wings, yet I can't help but wonder how. At any point the orbit is umbraic: *a lullaby of moths.* But is this what it means to consent to distance? What about ragstones, pillow & mantel, or the total number of trees? If houses are only fallen floors better imagined than described, then we mustn't misbelieve that casting phrases at the ceiling will hold the solution to glass.

Dear Peter,

Did I hear only a mumble &
a few distinct words

widening arches

or the inverse of wind

We met in annulment when
calm carried corpus or
assent calmed the crient
Because to interrogate nails

Without interrogating names
requires flowers made of stone
quarter-muds trenchantly dragged into dust
(an incomplete flower)

or cement below breath
or sentiment minus minutes

achieves a kind of sun
And what good is being invisible
or inside Avogadro's number
while parcels pension the nilpotent

Perhaps a bed born in diapause
or a few versts from the vacuole
if not a shadow . . . a curtain
piloting a shift to shore

Everything moans with breath
while your books

deprived of air

     dissolve

- Not Deliverable As Addressed
- Unable To Forward
- Insufficient Address
- Moved, Left No Address
- Unclaimed   • Refused
- Attempted—Not Known
- No Such Street   • Vacant
- No Such Number
- No Mail Receptacle
- Box Closed—No Order

WOODS HOLE MA 02543

if ever the shadow of snow
severed itself

to leave sutures out

or dacnicolor coils into
an attitude of light

only so even

peroneous anti-stones
step among the atmosphere

to disrobe the dream

pleas. A sexuality of space

Untie night's hands
at this hour

and remember rooms that
lost their will

In case you were wondering, it was blue

An act of silence
but I can't find an hour

or hairs to mimic desire
unless folded in fog

And to sleep parallel to the headboard
provides eyeless arteries

slightly obscured

a skeletal armature
too familiar to name

whenever we find it missing

Dear Peter,

Everything moans with breath unless acted upon, whether houses have only tents or boats made of dust. And the compass of a voice charts words for wounds, assumes its posture wearing a cape of water. But was it some spiderweb without lanterns as letters, lonely in its chamber? Or clock of ice carved with insinuation? You step away from the air and hardly wish it was. Yet I'm still trying to embrace the impalpable, as if it were a floating flower only a foot away.

at no instant have I described

windows that peel away a wall

or the sky color of carbon

because beyond these shadows

satellite or siderite

the eyes end of

a floating horizon
torn into

anfractuous flux

pillow despair
inside an elbow

clothed in sand

On the other side of
the alphabet

children are thought
to be shadows of rain

embracing efforts far
too fierce for their form

and unable to slip outside
their skin

into a voluptuous tower
traced with trees

they fall

from a canticle of dust
carving breath

into a sinuous whisper

Dear Peter,

Can you calculate an exact weight for a whisper? Is nudity a
form of dress? What does memory smell like, because I'm
still wondering about "meyer over monkey," and those
pen-shaped birds? Can you ride an umbrella out to sea? Are
the pajamas still unmailed? Would you say nets and fences
can be mirrors? How many fragments of fog scrape into trust?
If the counterpanes still leave me cold, is that trembling a song?
Do you think five minutes is enough, or did I step off the
platform a city too soon?

Or stood in a lane
Or dusk
Or it's possible

Or to react
Or lourd fardeau
Or plant

Or insistent streets
Or snake tapes
Or four-letter initials

Or if there's time
Or bearded
Or blankets

Or piano aprons
Or leaks
Or descending stirs

Or its end-product
Or sand cells
Or static

Or photograph food
Or bird
Or bauxite

Eventual Horizon

for Hildegard von Bingen

Eventual Horizon

____

there is no door, almost nothing, oblique figures

____

beneath the columns of flase marble

____

returned, removed, moonless as an estimate, circle dancing

____

like a mineral

____

possibly a raised sanctuary

____

verse 7 informed my lingering curiosity

____

pallor than grass

____

____

was not red (*J'ai ta lettre datée "En Mer"*)

____

minor litanies

misshapen pearl, problem or promise

walls & windows, crawling graveyards

Do not write this version.

The manuscript has been lying for centuries

groaned or grunted. passed on

was it Sappho or Telesilla

the space between *re-* and *in-*

a long-broken line.

is it or is it or not either

of some oblate vessel

of some ageless stone

alabaster or avenue

pressed perhaps, or rather

This will be counting.

This will be the blank new page

(C should have been inserted above)

compressed & chromatic, semi-tones & minor ninths, broken chords

polysemous, radiating. If there were

Two mirrors stare at each other

terse. ("a dactyl equals a spondee" or "one citadel equals two cities")

straight lines blocks boxes binds

models originally real deathless

---

the principal protagonist was never painted

---

forgotten or perhaps the opposite

---

reliquary jar in the shape of a jar

---

symphonies on a dead left hand

---

spent horses & hyphens

---

taut fibers

of nows millimetric measures reciprocal blues

equivocal and faint

with no organs

A child's dream of a mouth—fugue fingers

vertical to the horizon

(someone was mumbling about 76 ways of looking at a black word)

of the *no need of the moon to shine in it*

It was not a story to pass on.

mummified intact neutral tones in turn

moving towards

ALSO BY L ITMUS P RESS

Danielle Collobert, Notebooks: 1956-1978, trans. Norma Cole, $12
Aufgabe #1, eds. E. Tracy Grinnell & Peter Neufeld,
        with guest editors Norma Cole and Leslie Scalapino, $12
Aufgabe #2, ed. E. Tracy Grinnell,
        with guest editor Rosmarie Waldrop, $12
Aufgabe #3, ed. E. Tracy Grinnell,
        with guest editor Jen Hofer, $12
The House Seen from Nowhere, Keith Waldrop, $15